MR. ARCHIBALD FORBES

AND

THE ZULU WAR.

BY

N. L. WALFORD,

CAPTAIN ROYAL ARTILLERY,

INSTRUCTOR IN TACTICS, R. M. COLLEGE, SANDHURST.

The Naval & Military Press Ltd

Published jointly by

The Naval & Military Press Ltd

ZULULAND &c.

Scale. 15 Miles to 1 Inch.

Plan of Communications.

50 Miles to 1 Inch.

MR. FORBES AND THE ZULU WAR.

MR. FORBES is an entertaining person; but it may perhaps be doubted whether he is altogether capable of writing a "useful contribution to our critical military annals." He has the gift of employing powerful English to describe the various episodes of warfare. Marches, which to those engaged in them have appeared dull and wearisome, are by his magic pen made interesting and exciting. No one as he can hear the air "throb with the roar of the foe" when "the angry bullets are flying thick;" and indeed, but that there is for this statement Mr. Forbes's own authority, the expression would have appeared a little overstrained, referring as it does to an action which resulted in the loss (on our side) of ten killed and sixty wounded. But possibly Mr. Forbes's heart was with the Zulus at Ulundi, and it is Lord Chelmsford and the British army whom he intends to represent as his roaring

foe.   To speak seriously, Mr. Forbes is an excellent
war correspondent; the exploits of Captain A. and
Lieutenant B. lose nothing of their gallantry when
related by him; but "it is apparently not given"
to him to know that the power to delineate scenes
of horror and of blood in stirring words does not
necessarily imply any right to assume the position
of a military critic.   No one can deny the interest
excited by Mr. Forbes's correspondence during the
war of 1870 and in the late Russo-Turkish war;
but even the "foreign critics" who so anxiously
wait for his utterances must be slow to acknowledge the utility (from a " military " point of view)
of these fiery sketches, worked off at fever heat to
amuse a public which cares more for sensation than
for accurate criticism.   The opinion of the Con-
tinent may be unanimously in favour of Mr. Forbes's
knowledge of war, but it is to be feared that he has
very little (military) honour in his own country;
and I venture even to assert that, among officers
who have studied their profession, no importance
would be attached to the expression of Mr. Forbes's
adherence to either side of a disputed question. Even
the unfortunate "leading member of Lord Chelmsford's staff," who was so terribly snubbed when he
rashly ventured to ask " how I thought affairs were
proceeding," in all probability intended his question
merely as an act of courtesy, though, leaving Mr.

Forbes's presence a sadder and a wiser man, he must have determined for the future to confine his remarks to the conventional " Good-morning !" Mr. Forbes's courtesy and kindliness appear to be equalled only by his modesty and humour. His article might have been modelled on one of Napoleon's bulletins, it is so full of the monotonous " I ;" and when one has completed the study of his contribution to the *Nineteenth Century*, one sees, as if in a vision, Mr. Forbes disguised as Fame, with the eyes of the world upon him, crowning with one hand the grateful ghost of Wellington, while with the butt-end of his trumpet he pushes Lord Chelmsford into the darkness of limbo. Indeed, it is a curious matter to observe to what lengths an immoderate self-confidence may lead a man who has but little humour; for can anything be more comic than that Mr. Forbes should be good enough to give Lord Chelmsford a certificate as to his " gallant bearing " in action ? It is as if a Parliamentary reporter should say that Mr. Bright " has a very pretty knack of speaking." " *Ne sutor ultra crepidam* " is a motto which may be recommended to many critics, and " to be very wise after the event " has been a peculiarity of others than Lord Chelmsford.

It is an easy thing to find fault with the conduct of any past campaign; but all who read military history know well that the really difficult part of that study is to discover the causes for certain acts which on the face of them appear inexplicable. The time for the publication of the secret history of the Zulu war is yet far removed; but in the meanwhile, if Mr. Forbes cares to enter the back paths of military story, let him endeavour to unravel the mystery of Benedek's strategy in 1866.

Let me now pass on to review Mr. Forbes's criticisms, and consider his views as to the way in which the campaign should have been worked out.

I. "From the inception of the preparations up to and including the catastrophe of Isandlwana."

The task before Lord Chelmsford is well stated by Mr. Forbes :—With " 5,000 regular infantry, perhaps 1,500 irregular cavalry of varying efficiency," and 7,000 useless black troops, he had to invade a country defended by at least 40,000 warlike soldiers, inured to hardships, rapid in movement, and unencumbered with baggage, they being, in addition, the dread of their neighbours on account of their desperate bravery; but they had no firearms of any value.

Besides this task of invasion, Lord Chelmsford had to guard from counter-attack a line of from 150 to 200 miles of frontier, for at that period

(January, 1879) it was considered extremely probable that such a counter invasion would be made. Again, for reasons* beyond his control, though probably not those of which Mr. Forbes writes, the advance had to be commenced at a season of the year "when the ground is a quagmire, and every hill-torrent a river." Such conditions were truly hard, and Mr. Forbes says that a "strong general would have demurred to obey orders that committed him to an undertaking so manifestly precarious." I would wish to ask any soldier whether he is not of opinion that in that case the "strong general" should, and probably would, have been at once superseded by some one stronger than he? and we must earnestly hope that we may never see the day when an English officer, ordered on a definite duty, "demurs to obey" because an undertaking is dangerous, and persists in his "declinature" to move until he has under his command a force which he may consider sufficient to ensure success. Ought the garrison of Lucknow to have surrendered, since it was inade-

---

* One reason why the invasion took place at the commencement of the year was, that at that season the mealies, on which the Zulus principally depend for food, are so far from ripe that they cannot be gathered. If the enemy, thus dependent upon his stores of grain, could be forced to assemble and to remain under arms, it was probable that famine would soon compel his submission.

quate ? Was Rorke's Drift to be abandoned because the odds were thirty to one ? Is the siege of Sebastopol, where the besieged outnumbered the besiegers, in Mr. Forbes's eyes a military crime ? Then Agincourt was a mere waste of valuable lives, and Eyre's relief of Arrah was absolutely unpardonable.

Given that Lord Chelmsford's force was insufficient for the task allotted to it (as it undoubtedly was), the fault was not his, in that, obeying orders, he attempted, with so small an army, a task which others more remote from the scene of action judged to be less hard than it proved to be.

So much for the problem to be solved. Let us now compare the two plans which Mr. Forbes and Lord Chelmsford proposed to use.

Lord Chelmsford invaded Zululand in four columns as follows—Ulundi being the objective of the campaign :

1st. By Etshowe : strength, 1,600 white troops, under Col. Pearson.

2nd. By Middle Drift : under Col. Durnford.

3rd. By Rorke's Drift : strength, 2,000 white troops, under Col. Glyn.

4th. From Utrecht : strength, 1,800 white troops, under Col. Wood.

I have here taken no account of the numbers of the native troops, since, as Mr. Forbes rightly says, they were of dubious value. No. 2 column was, at an early period of the campaign, broken up, a portion being retained to occupy, on the defensive, the Umsinga Valley; while the remainder, with Colonel Durnford, joined No. 3 column on the 22nd January.

The action of these columns, according to Lord Chelmsford's plan, was to have been as follows: They were to advance a short distance into Zululand, establish a depôt and collect stores, and clear the intervening country by the action of detachments; this action tending to free the neighbourhood of the frontier of Natal from the presence of the enemy, whilst at the same time it would gradually drive the Zulus towards the north-east, and prepare the way for a decisive battle. Having provided for the safety of Natal by forcing away the neighbouring Zulus, and so establishing a safety zone, the several columns were to move forward another stage and repeat the process, until at last the enemy should be met in force. Mr. Forbes prefers the plan of invading on only two lines, as follows:

1st. By Etshowe;

2nd. From Utrecht;

and his objections to Lord Chelmsford's plan are:

i. The subdivision of the force and the consequent weakness of the columns.

The latter was the result of the small numbers of the invading army (and therefore beyond Lord Chelmsford's control), while the subdivision of the force was rendered necessary by the paramount consideration of observing the possible roads by which a counter-invasion might be made.

If Mr. Forbes's plan had been adopted, there would have remained a large intervening space, which could neither be cleared nor observed, but would have been available for use by the Zulu army, or even by a mere detachment of a few thousand men, who might easily have occasioned the retreat of the invaders by a sudden inroad into Natal. For this eventuality Mr. Forbes makes no provision, though in January, 1879, it was considered far from improbable, while Lord Chelmsford, to the best of his ability, considering his numerical weakness, guarded against it by using the intervening road from Rorke's Drift.

ii. The difficulty of intercommunication and mutual support.

This was due to the large extent of frontier to be covered, and to the consequent necessity of using convergent routes, and was further caused by the absence of roads, and by want of information as to the character of the country, which, in spite of Mr. Forbes's statement that "dozens of Natalians knew Zululand well," was very difficult to obtain from those whom he later calls "sparse visitors." This difficulty would have pressed even more heavily on the columns if they had been moved according to Mr. Forbes's plan, since the distance between the lines of advance would have been so much greater.

As regards the question of intercommunication, Lord Chelmsford actually met Colonel Wood after the passage of the frontier (on January 11th, on the Imkongani Hills), while Captain Barton re turned, on January 10th, to Bemba's Kop from Rorke's Drift. Such a meeting as the former, and any co-operation, would have been impossible if Mr. Forbes's plan had been followed. Mr. Forbes complains that "the British columns" were "standing around a great semicircle." Better so, surely, than if they had moved, as he proposes, along two lines nearly at right angles to each other.

iii. The question of "interior lines."

Mr. Forbes writes, on this question, of the Zulu army as if it were, like that of a European power, a coherent mass bound together by organisation, and amenable to discipline, whereas he must share the now common knowledge that after an action, whether victorious or not, the custom of the Zulus is to disperse. For example—after Isandlwana (22nd January), no force was available for attack on Colonel Wood until the 28th March, while further testimony to the fact can be found in the book lately published, called " Cetch-wayo's Dutchman." It is therefore idle to speak or write of "interior lines," since a motley and ill-disciplined rabble cannot be moved from point to point "to strike one column after another."

I hope that I have now shown, not that Lord Chelmsford's strategy was faultless (for he had so few troops that much had to be left to fortune), but that Mr. Forbes's plan, in place of being better than that of the General, merely exaggerates the faults of which he accuses Lord Chelmsford's com-bination, since the distances between the columns and the consequent failure of support would have been greater in the former than in the latter.

Mr. Forbes's next argument is, that "the event showed the faultiness of the strategy." All who have in any degree studied war, are aware that strategy depends for its eventual working-out upon tactical successes; and we claim that, in the pre-sent case, the plan fell through owing to the *tactical* failure at Isandlwana. But this I shall consider later, merely observing here that had the lines of invasion been limited to two, a tactical disaster would have been equally possible, if the other conditions of the fight at Isandlwana had been fulfilled.

The distance of Rorke's Drift from Durban was, we own, an objection to the route used; but if any communication whatever was to be kept up with No. 4 column, some such line must have been taken, at a greater distance from Durban than is the Lower Tugela.

On one point Mr. Forbes is absolutely incorrect, as he may himself discover by reference to a map of Zululand. Rorke's Drift is not a hundred, but ninety miles distant from Ulundi, while the Lower Tugela, stated by him to be seventy miles from that kraal, is, by way of Etshowe, about one hundred and six miles from it, so that in place of being farther, Rorke's Drift is a little nearer than Fort Tenedos* to the point in question.

But the relative amounts of these distances would not much affect the question, since Ulundi was not, like the capital of a civilised country, the heart of the people, whose capture is a national disaster; the Zulu army had to be met and defeated, it might be before Ulundi, it might be in any other place, that kraal having been taken as the objective only, in order to have a distinct plan, while the general scheme of the campaign was liable to alteration according to circumstances.

The argument as to the "undue prolongation of

* Of the character of the road from Etshowe to Ulundi we shall speak on a subsequent page.

the columns (which, *pace* Mr. Forbes, is not expressed by the word " friction") was, in spite of his assertion to the contrary, a strong one, for it was considered probable that the Zulus, if well advised, would certainly delay and obstruct the advance of our troops by frequent and desultory attacks on the baggage train. That they did not do this must be ascribed to their habit of fighting only savages who have no train; but no one even now can doubt but that, if properly worked, a series of such enterprises, carried out by determined men, would have harassed our troops more than ten such fights as Ulundi or Kambula, and to the Zulus' neglect to take advantage of such a course must be ascribed our ultimate success.

A line of six hundred waggons, such as Colonel Wood conducted, in June 1879, to the Upoko river, has, in single file, a length of about thirteen miles. What Afghan tribe would allow such a convoy to pass scot-free?

Mr. Forbes next writes of the later experience of " Wood and Newdigate." He gives us no date, but, assuming that he refers to the month of May or June, no one can know better than he that the conditions of transport in these months were very different to what they were in January—as to the state of the road, the ambulance of forage, the amount of water in the rivers, etc."

"Active hostilities opened on the 11th of January."

Mr. Forbes asserts that the fact that a delay of No. 3 column was necessary for road-making, is in itself condemnatory of the line of advance selected ; but whatever line had been chosen the road must have been prepared for the passage of waggons, and even that on Etshowe, which Mr. Forbes considers should have been used as a main line of invasion, is spoken of as follows, by Colonel Pearson : " The road to Ekowe from the Tugela is a mere beaten track, and at this season of the year very bad in places, especially this side of the Inyazani, which is often very steep, narrow, and sloping towards the valley (where cut on the side of a hill), thus rendering a waggon liable to upset. The latter defect we remedied *en route;* but as there is no stone in the country, I am afraid it will never be possible to do more than for each convoy to repair the road for itself. There is nothing to repair it with except logs and brushwood, which of course won't stand the traffic of a large number of waggons."

There is one other reason than "God's providence" why Pearson's column might not have been annihilated on its march to Etshowe by the "massed Zulu army" three days earlier (19th January) than Isandlwana; and this is, that by the itinerary of the Zulu forces, it appears that at that

date the 20,000 men, who went to Isandlwana, were
at Isipize, and the 4,000 who attacked Pearson on
the 22nd at Undini, the remainder of the army
being with the king; while Pearson on the 19th
was south of the Inyezani river, and therefore
separated by about fifty miles of impassable bush
from the "massed Zulu army," and by about the
same distance from Ulundi and the king.   Again,
it is certain that, in accordance with the known
custom of the Zulus of dispersing after an action,
if Pearson had been attacked, whether successfully
or not, there could have been no force available for
the onslaught on Glyn's column, in which case, probably, Mr. Forbes would have written that
"God's providence" had preserved the latter
force.   The direct interposition of Providence to
save Pearson implies that the destruction of the
force at Isandlwana was also the act of God, and
therefore beyond the power of man to avert.
This can scarcely be what Mr. Forbes wishes to
suggest.

In order to save time and space, I am willing
(under protest), for purposes of argument, to accept
Mr. Forbes's statement that the position of the
camp at Isandlwana was "inherently vicious,"
merely asking him that he will kindly explain
what bearing this fact (if it is one) can possibly
have on the result of an action which was fought

out at a distance of at least half a mile from that camp? But on two points I do not hesitate distinctly to contradict Mr. Forbes. Lord Chelmsford did *not* select the site of the camp; the officer who did so is well known, and acknowledges the fact of his having chosen the spot, which neither he nor anyone else considered to be at all unsuited to a camp. Again, neither Glyn nor Dartnell made any "representations" to Lord Chelmsford on the subject of the "fire-zone," while if the former had objected to the site, it was at any time in his power to change it. It is true that neither of these facts are of the least consequence from a military point of view, but they serve to show that Mr. Forbes is sometimes inaccurate. That he should be mistaken in this instance is not wonderful, as he was not in Africa at the time of which he writes so dogmatically; but it should be a warning to him for the future to distinguish clearly between what he knows and what he has merely heard.

Again, as to the construction of the camp. Mr. Forbes considers that either an entrenchment or a laager should have been made, and in that view he is supported by paragraphs 19 and 20 of the Regulations issued by Lord Chelmsford, which are too long for quotation. But he entirely mistakes the object and use of these defences; and

2

the experience of Ulundi, with the opinion of many officers who were in Zululand, leads us to the belief that, if proper tactical dispositions had been made, the force left at Isandlwana could have dispensed with entrenchments or a laager. One thing we are prepared to acknowledge, namely, that any arrangement which would have tended to keep the defending force near to its ammunition and in a closed body, would have been of unmixed advantage.

1st. As to an entrenchment; that is, a ditch and parapet.

A ditch is used to provide earth for the parapet, and is never (in field-works) of sufficient depth to form an impassable obstacle against an assault. A parapet is intended to cover the defenders from fire, and is but a small obstacle to a charge, which must be prevented or repulsed by the fire of the garrison. Given that a parapet eight feet high and a ditch ten feet deep could have been made in the time, what obstacle would they together have offered to a Zulu rush ? Their use would have been (i.) to give confidence to the men ; (ii.) to prevent the dissemination of the force. The real defence lay, and must always lie, in the fire of the defenders, and their strength, (as is evident from the battle of Tashkessen in 1877,) is in direct ratio to their supply of ammunition, while a parapet serves only to diminish casualties from fire. The Zulu fire was contemptible, their charge redoubtable ; cover was not needed for the one, and would have been useless against the other.

2nd. As to a laager formation.

This is a defence formed of waggons interlocked, and is a Boer artifice, suited to their irregular mode of fighting, but even with them used principally to protect the oxen. The space contained is small in proportion to the number of waggons which surround it,* and the defence is in consequence usually conducted from the outside. It may be doubted whether a laager made with the waggons at Isandlwana would have held the whole force, including as it did artillery and cavalry, as well as the transport oxen. At Gingihlovo the laager was covered by a small parapet, and served in some way as a citadel ; at Kambula, the laager was subsidiary to the parapet ; while at Ulundi, the fighting was done in the open without parapet or laager, the latter being used merely to cover the camp, and this, though formed of the whole of the waggons, was small enough to be held by one battalion.

---

* A round laager of fifty-two waggons, and a square laager of sixty-four waggons, will each just hold its own cattle. A smaller convoy than the former cannot make a perfect laager.

A laager, if it had existed, must have been defended from the outside, and might *not have prevented* the dispersion of the troops, while a parapet, useful only as a means of concentrating the defence, must have forfeited even that advantage as soon as the troops left the camp.

The day of Isandlwana, January 22nd, 1879.

Lord Chelmsford, accompanied by half of Colonel Glyn's column, moved off about 4 a.m., leaving in the camp, " regarding the safety of which he had no misgivings," 750 Europeans and 400 natives.* The orders for the protection of the said camp " emanated" (as they should) from the staff officer of Colonel Glyn, who was therefore obviously in command of the column.   The *written* orders contained these words, " Draw in your camp, or your line of defence," it is uncertain which.   In thus moving, Lord Chelmsford was adopting the very mode of advance suggested by Mr. Forbes in· an earlier portion of his article, namely, the successive march of fractions of the force at a day's interval. But perhaps the instructor blames the scholar for having foreseen his proposal.

To this Mr. Forbes would probably make two objections ; first, that the Zulus were so near that the march was not advisable ; and second, that

* Afterwards joined by Colonel Durnford, with about 450 men, white and black.

this mode of advance was to be used only when each force was capable of defending itself.

1st. The distance of the Zulu army on the morning of the 22nd January. This Mr. Forbes gives as one mile and a half. This statement *is utterly inaccurate*, and for it Mr. Forbes has no authority but the evidence of a native, who was unlikely to be a computer of distance in English measures. An officer who was present with Colonel Glyn's force, and had reconnoitred the ground, gives it as his opinion that the Zulu camp was seven miles, and the spot where Colonel Durnford commenced to fight five miles, from Isandlwana. An officer of the Royal Engineers, who surveyed the ground, found that the latter point was just under four miles from the camp, and agrees that seven miles was the distance of the Zulu bivouac.

This force Lord Chelmsford intended to fight.

2nd. This is the point, the whole soul of the question.

Was the force left at Isandlwana capable, without assistance, of repulsing any attack made on it ?

I answer unhesitatingly that it was ; and that it would have done so, but for the fatal tactical fault of fighting in an extended line,* and for the

* South African correspondence, *Daily Telegraph*, Feb. 13, 1880 : "Two miles off, on the left front, the missing com. panies of the 24th were discovered ; and on the right front, a

administrative failure in the supply of ammunition.

The evidence of Captain Essex before the Court of Inquiry is proof that the early attacks (which should never have been made) were carried out in extended order : "When under the inexorable necessity of battle the troops had been forced into the proper square formation, no ammunition was procurable." *

A mode of attack which the Prussian soldier found by experience to be the best for fire against fire, was used by our men for fire against charge, and we have learnt at great and sad cost how entirely circumstances may alter cases.

Restoring the words omitted by Mr. Forbes from Lord Chelmsford's despatch, we may say, " Had the force in question but taken up a defensive position *in the camp itself*,"† there can be little doubt but that they would have repulsed all

---

similar distance away, bodies were found lying thick in the grass." This was, indeed, extended order.

* We are informed that boxes of ammunition having been brought up, it was found impossible to open them, the tools provided for that purpose being in camp.

† With regard to the statement in Lord Chelmsford's despatch, "The oxen were yoked three hours before the attack took place," Mr. Forbes entirely fails to grasp its meaning, owing to his ignorance that to inspan the oxen would be the first step towards constructing a laager, since the waggons could not be dragged into place by hand.

attacks, since, even as it was, the Zulus acknowledge that they were on the point of retreating
before the remnant who survived, and would have
done so, but for the cessation of the fire owing to
the want of ammunition, and the consequent retirement towards the camp.

Supposing that they had so retreated, we may
perhaps consider that the advance towards Ulundi
would have been virtually unopposed, and the
campaign ended in a few weeks or even days ; in
which case Lord Chelmsford would probably have
been declared by his "military critics" to be in no
way entitled to praise for a success which was
obtained in his absence.

The defence of Rorke's Drift was a gallant act,
and doubtless saved Natal from a Zulu raid ; but
is not some share of the praise lavished on its
defenders due to the man who placed the post
where it was of so great utility ?

Are all failures to be visited on Lord Chelmsford, and all successes to be declared to be due
to others ? and when a *tactical* disaster has
destroyed a carefully prepared plan of campaign,
should blame be given to the head which formed
the plan, or to the hands which failed to carry it
out ? "De mortuis nil nisi bonum" is a high and
Christian maxim ; but do not let us tear down the
well-earned reputation of the living, in order to

build up from the fragments a poor monument to the dead.

One question remains, which we must ask Mr. Forbes to answer :—Where does he find, and what is his authority for the statement, that to omit to make a camp defensible in face of an enemy in force is a violation of the " most rudimentary principles of warfare " ? and will he kindly quote one example of a case where this *rule* has been observed, at least since the beginning of the century ? The days of fortified camps are long past, except under the conditions of a siege.

II. "The second period of the operations extended from Isandlwana to the commencement of the final invasion."

" The early days of this period," Mr. Forbes says, "were spent in aimless despondency." In answer to this, it is proposed to show the work done during the month of February. On the 1st, Colonel Buller destroyed the Magulusi military kraal ; on the 10th, the same gallant officer captured 490 head of cattle on the Inhlobane Mountain ; on the 15th, a party sent by Colonel Wood defeated a Zulu raid ; Colonel Wood himself, during the month, prepared the position at Kambula, and prevented the Zulus from making incursions on the north-west ; on the 1st of March, Colonel Pearson de-

stroyed Dabulamanzi's kraal. Surely this is not
altogether aimless despondency? Anxiety there may
well have been, since Lord Chelmsford now found
himself committed to the defence of some 200 miles
of frontier with a force of less than 3,000 men, not
including Pearson's column, which was shut up in
Etshowe.   To anyone who looks back upon and
considers the terrible position of Natal at this date,
it will appear only natural that Lord Chelmsford
should feel himself grievously oppressed by the
weight of his responsibility.   The possessions and
lives of many thousand fellow-creatures were
dependent (as it seemed) on his power to restrain,
with a mere handful of troops, a numerous and
jubilant enemy, as ruthless in rapine as they were
brave in combat.   Surely here was cause for cease-
less anxiety and unwearied watching, leaving little
taste or time for a useless examination into the
causes of past events.   More evidence was, however,
forwarded at a later date (under cover of a letter of
February 9th), and it is evident that if the higher
authorities of the Army had considered the Court
of Inquiry such a "solemn mockery," the question
might easily have been re-opened, since the result
of this description of court, unlike that of a court-
martial, does not bar further proceedings.

But I have no intention of following Mr. Forbes
into questions of administration, since, contrary to

his apparent opinion, they form no part of a military criticism.

The "true and trenchant quotation" which Mr. Forbes inserts makes two statements, which contrast strangely with his own. How shall we reconcile "Colonel Wood is completely isolated and *en l'air*," and "Wood, reinforced by the 80th, was available for invasive purposes," except on the supposition that the advent of a single battalion had power to advance his attitude from that of the feebly defensive to that of strenuous offence?

Again, the "true and trenchant" says :— "Colonel Pearson's fate quivers in the balance;" while on the next page Mr. Forbes writes, "Pearson was quite safe behind his entrenchment," and proceeds to show that, at the time of the relief, the garrison of Etshowe was in good health and on full rations,* though during the interval no supplies or reinforcements had been received by them. The true and trenchant paragraph quoted must have been written by some one suffering sadly from the despondency which Mr. Forbes deprecates.

The relief of Etshowe was successful, and even Mr. Forbes records that the Zulus at Gingilhovo received a crushing repulse; but he urges, in that

---

* With a long sick list, Colonel Pearson had run short of many of the medicines most required, and had reported that his provisions would last to the end of March only.

generous and courteous style which is so peculiarly
his own, that Lord Chelmsford " remained obtuse
to encouragements which would have surely stimu-
lated most men to enterprise." The Zulus, having
been scattered and demoralised by the defeats of
Kambula and Gingilhovo, Mr. Forbes considers
that Lord Chelmsford, " with bare necessaries for a
month " (if he could have carried them), should
have pressed only "forced marches" (over a new
and trackless country) to Ulundi, and further
asserts that Lord Chelmsford retired in five
marches from Etonganeni to Etshowe. The facts
are as follows : The flying column marched from
Etonganeni to St. Paul's in six days (during one of
which there was a halt) ; the road falls 2000 feet
in the interval ; and Etshowe is twenty-two miles
from St. Paul's. Again, according to Mr. Forbes,
Colonel Clarke's column reached Etonganeni in a
few days. As a matter of fact, the march extended
over thirteen days, viz., from July 24th to August
6th. The distance covered was seventy-two miles.
Again there was no transport available for the car-
riage of supplies.* But given that the force had
reached Ulundi in a week, what would Lord
Chelmsford have found there ? Nothing !

The march was not impossible, though it must
have been difficult ; but would probably have led

---

* The contracts having expired.

only to the finding of Ulundi deserted, in which case the army must have again retired to obtain the bare necessaries for another month. So far from being "master of the situation,"* Lord Chelmsford would probably have found himself alone, and committed to jungle warfare in the Ngomé forest. He might have been reinforced and reprovisioned from "behind," Mr. Forbes writes; but it passes the power of man to imagine how he could have been so supported; and, even if that point be allowed, he certainly could neither have been supplied with cavalry, nor have captured Cetchwayo with dismounted men. Whether Mr. Forbes's plan be good or not, it is probably fortunate that Lord Chelmsford did not adopt it, as he thus gave time to the Zulu army to reassemble and eventually to be defeated *en masse*, in place of being hunted in detail, while he himself was enabled to organise his forces and transport for the final march. Failing this movement, which, we may mention, must necessarily have been unsupported by Colonel Wood, Mr. Forbes considers that Lord Chelmsford should have held Etshowe in place of Gingilhovo. To this there is a sufficient answer in the fact that fifteen miles of road,

---

* Will Mr. Forbes kindly explain the wonderful sentence which begins, "Not much bracing of that nervous system," etc., and ends—nowhere !

Emprise.—Attempt of *danger*. Undertaking of *hazard.*—*Johnson's Dictionary.* Not exactly what Mr. Forbes intends to convey.

swampy, hilly, and rough in various parts along its whole length, intervened between the two posts. This distance, inconsiderable to an advancing army which has but once to traverse it, becomes of great account with regard to the repeated journeys of transport oxen. If the post of Gingilhovo was "futile," how could that at Etshowe have been more useful, while it is certain that the former was far easier to supply than the latter would have been?

III. "The third period extends from the relief of Etshowe to the combat of Ulundi."

But perhaps it will be as well to consider, first, the remarks made by Mr. Forbes upon Lord Chelmsford's staff, as otherwise to do so would interrupt the tale of the proceedings. He complains that Lord Chelmsford would have no Chief of the Staff. Mr. Forbes writes as if this omission showed wanton perverseness on the part of Lord Chelmsford, in that he absolutely refused a lieutenant, whom modern warfare has shown to be of "inestimable value." We do not deny the desirability of such an adjunct, but it has not been one usually attached to British generals; and if Mr. Forbes will search through our military history, though he may pick up many crumbs by the way, he will find but one instance of a Chief of the Staff up to the year 1879. Nor is any such

officer included in the list of the staff of a *General*,
so that it is, to say the least, improbable that one
would have been allowed to *Lieutenant-General*
Lord Chelmsford.

Mr. Forbes says that the force in Zululand was
virtually an army corps; he computes it at over
20,000 men, but probably does not mean to imply
that it so much exceeded that number as to amount
to 37,000 men, which is the strength of an army
corps. Of this 20,000 he states that only 14,000
were whites, having previously qualified all black
troops as "trash;" so that, by Mr. Forbes's own
showing, Lord Chelmsford had at this time under
his command but little more than one-third of
an army corps at war strength. The officers (or
shall we, *more* Mr. Forbes, say "persons"?) of
Lord Chelmsford's staff, individually attacked,
may be left to defend themselves; but even an
"unofficial person" should know that he wanders
from the path of military criticism when he con-
descends to confuse amiability in a staff officer
with his fitness for his duties, and jocosely denies
the existence of the one by way of proving the
absence of the other.

On one point with regard to the Staff Mr. Forbes
is strangely ignorant, since he appears not to be
aware that, by the present organisation of the
Army, the offices and duties of the Adjutant-

general's and Quarter-master-general's depart-
ments are amalgamated, while the Intelligence
officer discharges that portion of the latter's work
which deals with information and reconnaissance.
In the next sentence, Mr. Forbes's words, if taken
literally, produce a very erroneous idea of the
facts, for there is no reason to believe that " the
poor lad who fell at Ityotyosi river, and the man
who left him to his fate " were sole representatives,
or representatives at all, of the Intelligence branch
of Lord Chelmsford's staff.   Mr. Forbes should
know that there were many other officers so employed, and ought to be aware that the expression
" casual service " does them great and unmerited
wrong, though perhaps he may not even guess how
entirely so careless a statement alienates from him
all trust and credit.   It would be satisfactory to
learn whether Mr. Forbes makes this assertion on
the authority of the *ad interim* Quarter-master-
general.

   That Lord Chelmsford's Intelligence officer
should know little of the tract through which the
army was to march is not surprising, since only
Zulus had any knowledge of the road, and the
opinion of a Zulu on the question of transport
would have little practical value ; but that he
should have unbosomed himself to such an extent
as Mr. Forbes asserts, shows that Lord Chelms-

ford's staff were ignorant that any careless remarks which they might make would be inevitably used as literary capital by the Universal Military Critic. Let this be a warning to staff officers to combine for the future, according to the good old rule, affability and reticence, and to limit their discourse with " unofficial persons," especially of a literary type, to "Yea, yea !" and " Nay, nay !"

Though brigadiers have been, not unfrequently, detached during the advance of an army, the general in question will scarcely thank Mr. Forbes for calling attention to the fact that such was his fate. Save us from our friends ! and from other people's " detractors."

We come now to the list of offices which Mr. Forbes states to have been united in the person of Lord Chelmsford.

" Chief of the staff" we have already answered.

" Divisional-general and brigadier." In his remarks as to the time preceding the battle of Isandlwana, Mr. Forbes gives, as an article of accusation against Lord Chelmsford, that he did not personally order the entrenchment of that camp. But would not this have been to take the command out of Colonel Glyn's hand, and to have essayed to be his own brigadier ? Blame, and blame always, from Mr. Forbes, whatever Lord Chelmsford does, or leaves to others to do.

" Sergeant-major, road-mender, ox-driver, and mealie-cob-collector," mean, we presume, nothing more than that Lord Chelmsford's zeal with regard to discipline, roads, transport and supply, appeared to Mr. Forbes to be excessive. That it did so appear, is probably due less to Lord Chelmsford's ubiquity than to Mr. Forbes's want of knowledge as to the paramount necessity of incessant supervision which is incumbent on the commander of an army, who too often, if he wants anything done, must do it or see it done himself. But to save argument, let us own that Lord Chelmsford gave care too vigilant and unceasing to the working of every department of his force; even then we, who are not military critics, feel that this was a fault on the right side, and one not altogether deserving of so witty and facetious a catalogue.

This portion of Mr. Forbes's article, writ short, possibly means merely that Lord Chelmsford and his staff did not admire, and perhaps did not please Mr. Forbes, who is anxious to borrow the motto of his country's thistle, " Nemo me impune lacessit," and to show that, as he puts it, he will " take dunts frae naebody." Affability and reticence, Messieurs the Staff-officers, must be your rule : affability to " detractors " and reticence to " unofficial persons."

The charges which Mr. Forbes brings against
Lord Chelmsford, with regard to the third period
of the campaign, are connected with the following
subjects :

(i.) The stay of the 1st Division on the Tugela.

(ii.) The direction and plan of the advance into
Zululand.

(iii.) The delay of that advance (with a proposed
plan).

(iv.) The tactics at Ulundi.

These, with Mr. Forbes's incidental grumblings,
we propose to examine in the above order.

(i.) This charge, stated in the words of the
article, is as follows : " 6,500 men, comprising the
1st Division, under General Crealock, Lord
Chelmsford, according to his own statement,
deliberately pigeon-holed on and about the Lower
Tugela, restrained* from discretional offensive,
and inoperative, from its position, for the defence
of the long frontier line."

Before examining this question, we should
wish to draw attention, in connection with the
word "deliberately," to the following extracts
from the two succeeding pages of Mr. Forbes's
article :

"I have information from a source entitled to

* Query, the Tugela ?

implicit credence that Lord Chelmsford 'left the 1st Division entirely to the independent direction of its general.' "*

" It was Lord Chelmsford's intention . . . . to give the hand to Crealock, and to advance on Ulundi in co-operation with him."†

" Crealock should be told that either he must advance, or," etc.

" There remains but to dismiss the 1st Division as a non-efficient factor, *intentionally or unintentionally* so on Lord Chelmsford's part, in the scheme," etc.

What are we to make of this? Little more we think than the undeniable fact that the 1st Division did remain on the Lower Tugela, not for three (as Mr. Forbes states) but for two months; namely, from about the 20th of April, when General Crealock took command, to the middle of June, at which date a considerable portion of his force was north of the Inyezani river. But to whom Mr. Forbes imputes blame for this delay, it is impossible to discover, and indeed it is not easy to say why blame should be imputed at all. If General Crealock had wished, or had been ordered to move, the mortality among his transport oxen

---

* This information was correct.
† This is a mistake on Mr. Forbes's part.

was so great,* that he could not have advanced in
any great strength.   But if, on the other hand
Lord Chelmsford chose to leave a portion of his
force in reserve, or to retain it in a position to
cover Durban from a counter-attack, what rule of
war would he break in either case? and if
General Crealock, finding time hang heavy on his
hands, occupied himself in the manner so humor-
ously and delicately described by Mr. Forbes,
surely no harm was done, and indeed many
generals have gone to their graves full of honour
who have performed less useful work.   But nothing
seems to please Mr. Forbes.   He blames Lord
Chelmsford for leaving instructions ("if indeed
there were any") that the 1st Division were to
remain on the Tugela, and in the next paragraph
"ventures respectfully to question Lord Chelmsford's expression of his deliberate intention to
dispense with the co-operation of his 1st Division
in offensive operations," giving two reasons for
doing so : 1st. The word of Lord Chelmsford himself, which he has already doubted, and (apparently
in contrast) information from an anonymous source
entitled to implicit credence ; and, 2nd. His own
affirmation, apparently introduced to lead up to an
anecdote concerning the adventures of an "un-

* I am told, on good authority, that 1,200 oxen died in ten
days.

official person," who as closely resembles Mr. Forbes as Philip drunk resembles Philip sober.

We find, here, blame for keeping the 1st Division idle, blame for proposing to advance it, and blame (joined with despairing entreaty) for the supposed desire of Lord Chelmsford to wait for the said advance.

What deduction can we draw from the above except this, that Mr. Forbes, burning to strike something or somebody, a very " Ghazi " of litera-ture, is bent on running amuck through the Army List.

We may dismiss Mr. Forbes's "authoritative critic" with the following paraphrase, which pro-bably expresses what was in his mind : " I am discontented with my present post, and wish that I had Crealock's division.   In that case I would do anything, right or wrong, which might serve to prevent the 2nd Division from having all the fun to themselves.   Life is very dull in Natal, and even if I could not rush forward to the king's kraal I should at least get out of this place."

The "damnable iteration of vague accusations' we may pass over, as well as the conversation with " a leading member of Lord Chelmsford's staff," who is introduced as a sort of pantaloon to Mr. Forbes's clown, in order that he may be bullied and (morally) knocked about by the latter.   Indeed, the whole of Mr. Forbes's article reminds one dimly of the ancient drama of Mr. Punch, with its one character, spouting his own praises in a monotonous squeak, and summarily disposing of any other puppet who may, for the moment, have been permitted to share the stage with him. Let us not pursue the parallel further, for, though his high-handed mode of dealing unofficially with official persons was both rigorous and successful, Mr. Punch's final end was sad, and, we hope, not ominous.

(ii.) The direction of the advance on Ulundi.

The gist of the accusation which is contained in this portion of Mr. Forbes's article is, that Lord Chelmsford clung to the policy of invading Zululand "from round the corner." "With a force (now) strong enough for the double duty of defence and of invasion," Lord Chelmsford provided for both by his recurrence to his original plan of moving on three lines, while he observed the intervening country by detached bodies of troops echeloned along the frontier. Mr. Forbes, unable to follow the object of this divided advance, declares that the duty of the defence was "shunned;" but, as I have before endeavoured to show (with reference to the first invasion), by the very direction of his advance Lord Chelmsford covered a large portion of the frontier. Besides, by this time the fear of invasion had passed, since the few raids which were made into Natal were repulsed by the native forces.

Mr. Forbes writes of the "South-western angle of Zululand" as being, of all points along the frontier, the most remote from Ulundi. Does he refer to Rorke's Drift, to Koppie Allein, or to Landman's Drift? in either case the following list of distances, taken from the Triangulation of the country, may serve to show that his statement is inaccurate :

Fort Tenedos to Ulundi (by way of Etshowe and St. Paul's), 106 miles. Durban is about 70 miles from Tenedos.

Landman's Drift to Ulundi (by way of Koppie Allein and Fort Evelyn, 106 miles. Dundee is 11½ miles from Landman's Drift.

Koppie Allein to Ulundi is 82½ miles.

Rorke's Drift to Ulundi (by the map), about 90 miles.

The road from Etshowe to Ulundi is a one-waggon track, and its character may be judged from the following facts : The train which accompanied Colonel Wood's column on its return march, left camp at 7 a.m. on the 15th of July, moving on St. Paul's, at which point the last waggon arrived at 10 p.m. ; it thus required fifteen hours to move seven miles downhill.

Colonel Clarke, advancing in light order from

Port Durnford to Ulundi, occupied an entire day on the march between the Umvaloosi and St. Paul's, a distance of five miles.   In the last two miles of this stage there is a rise of 800 feet !

Such is the road which Mr. Forbes asserts should have been used for the main line of invasion. The fact that he had never seen and knew nothing of this road, at once excuses and condemns him.

On the line actually used, by the Upoko river, the waggons moved five abreast, thus diminishing the length of a column of 600 teams from thirteen miles to two and a half miles ; this fact, assuming the rate of march to be two and a half miles per hour, would cause a saving of about four hours in each day's march.

Again, Mr. Forbes objects to the selection of a " place called Dundee " as the starting-point for the column, on the ground that it is two hundred miles from Durban, but he forgets that the latter was neither the only source of supplies nor the principal source of transport.   It is true that from it came preserved meats, biscuits, medical stores, boots, clothing, ammunition and other European productions ; but the more bulky stores, such as mealies and forage, and also the cattle,* were col-

---

* And waggons, of which the majority came from the Free State, to which Dundee is nearer than is Durban by one hundred miles.

lected from the country ; while, given that an army draws to itself supplies in an equal ratio from every quarter (as it will approximately), a force stationed inland is supplied from a circle, that on the sea-coast from a semicircle ; from this it results that though European stores would not have been brought up to Dundee, yet native supplies must have been carried to Durban, if the latter had been used as the only base. It was, therefore, probably wiser, though the operation (owing to the character of the transport) occupied a great length of time, to prepare another depôt near the frontier, and to use that as a new or secondary base.

There was further the strategical plan of the campaign to be considered, and Mr. Forbes should be the first to award praise to Lord Chelmsford for selecting a line of advance within easy reach of Wood's column, since in the earlier portion of the article he speaks so bitterly against dissemination of forces, etc. We cannot doubt but that these paramount considerations of supply and strategy led Lord Chelmsford to select Dundee as his starting-point, and to disregard the two hundred miles of road which are such a stumbling-block to Mr. Forbes.

The example which Mr. Forbes gives would be more exact if we suppose the " circumambulator

of the Green Park" to wish to take with him to
Stafford House a book which he had left at the
Wellington Barracks ; in that case we maintain he
would pass Buckingham Palace on his way.

Our objection to Mr. Forbes's proposed plan of
invasion by the Lower Tugela is the same as we
gave before; namely, that unless there were in
addition an intervening column, it would be
utterly impossible to hold out the hand to Colonel
Wood's force, while the distance to be traversed
we have shown was equally great.   Again, we may
ask, since General Crealock's division could not
collect from the district of the Tugela sufficient
transport for itself alone, how could a yet larger
army have been supplied ?

Mr. Forbes next speaks of the "common weakness" of Colonel Wood's and General Newdigate's
force.   The former had, on the 23rd of June, 3,374
men, and the latter 5,025 men.*   Colonel Wood
was therefore as strong, and General Newdigate
far stronger than was Lord Chelmsford after the
relief of Etshowe, when, according to Mr. Forbes,
he should have marched directly on Ulundi.

The final abandonment of that which Mr. Forbes
calls " the only good strategical feature in Lord
Chelmsford's original dispositions "—namely, an

---

* These numbers are from an official telegram to the High
Commissioner.

advance from Utrecht—was wise, since it had been found by experience that, after an action, the Zulu army invariably broke up, and it was therefore unnecessary to hold a force in readiness to cut off its retreat, since as a body it would have ceased to exist, while no amount of care could have prevented individuals from passing the frontier. Besides, Swaziland did not, at this time, offer a very tempting refuge to a Zulu rival, destitute of cattle, and sunk from an object of fear to one of contemptuous hatred.

That Lord Chelmsford, in his advance, selected the line by Landman's Drift in place of that by Rorke's Drift, should be a subject of delight to Mr. Forbes, since this choice had the effect of bringing him nearer to Colonel Wood's column, and prevented the "subdivision of the force."

We have now to make a grave accusation against Mr. Forbes. Lord Chelmsford, from above the Jackal's Neck camp, may possibly have seen Etshowe ; but how many of the men who were at that point on the 4th of April were at the Jackal's Neck on the 27th of June ? We answer, not one company, nor, with the exception of the staff, do we believe that there was one man.

What does Mr. Forbes mean, then, by writing of "marching a division . . . round eleven-twelfths of a circle," when he should know that all the troops who were present at Gingilhovo and Etshowe were, on the 27th of June, still in that part of Zululand. The battalions in Etshowe were " The Buffs " and 99th. Those which relieved Etshowe were the 57th, the 60th, the 91st, and detachments of " The Buffs " and 99th. These troops afterwards formed the 1st Division, and had not moved to Dundee, nor was any part of them present at the Jackal's Neck.

Mr. Forbes's paragraph is so worded, that, owing to the ambiguity which permits that the name of a general may mean, either him personally, or the force of which he is the head, it would appear to anyone who did not know, or did not care to search for the facts, as if the troops which relieved, or had served in Etshowe, had been marched *viâ* Dundee to the Jackal's Neck. No division " with its huge supplies," nor even a battalion, had been so marched ; and we prefer to assume that Mr. Forbes is entirely ignorant of the movements of the troops during the campaign, rather than believe that he intended to convey an utterly false impression. Shade of Shakespeare! To think that a man should venture to use that name, who has such a load of crass criticism on his literary loins, scarcely, surely, to be alleviated by arduous alliteration!

" From that height, too," may have been visible

the sea near Port Durnford,* but, in spite of Mr.
Forbes's statement that stores were being landed
there on the 27th of June, as a matter of fact the
port was not opened until the 30th of June, nor
even then was communication between the ships
and the shore always easily carried on, as Sir Garnet
Wolseley discovered, when, after waiting during the
2nd and 3rd of July, he was prevented by the surf
from landing, and compelled to return to Durban.

(iii.) The delay in the advance : with a plan of
alternative procedure propounded by "one who
knows war well." Mr. Forbes accuses Lord Chelmsford of unnecessary delay, and in an unsavoury sentence implies that sanitary arrangements did not
meet with the same attention from General
Newdigate as from General Crealock. We may be
permitted, perhaps, to neglect the latter part of
the charge, and to examine only the former.

The watchword was to be "Advance! advance!
advance!"

"Yes, advance, if only for a few miles, into the
enemy's country; advance our infantry to ports
safely (?) established on Zulu soil;" and in a few
days we should have heard of a new disaster.

The infantry was to be sent on "with small
convoys . . . . with strong escorts." How long
would a strong escort have required in order to

* Fifty miles distant, as the crow flies, and about seventy
by road. This, Mr. Forbes calls "five marches."

eat all the food carried by a small convoy, and
what depôts could have been formed, unless of
empty biscuit-tins and mealie-bags ? As far as it
is possible to follow this remarkable plan, "one
who knows war well" proposed to send forward
detachments of infantry, without any preliminary
cavalry reconnaissance, blindfolded into Zululand,
each detachment being accompanied by a supply of
food, ammunition and arms, presumably for the
aid of the distressed Zulus ; into their hands, at
least, all must have eventually fallen. This may
be philanthropy (of a kind), but it is not war.
And what, we may ask, is the meaning of "chopping
up forces," "subdivision of the force," "unsoldier-
like subdivision," and "individual weakness of
the columns," if these terms are not to be applied
to the ridiculous plan of one who may "know war
well," but has certainly not the vaguest idea of how
to conduct it ?

"One would indeed then have felt that one was
doing something," and something absurdly wrong ;
"not indeed eating up more stores or wasting
more money," but offering up detachments of
British soldiers as a sacrifice to the great, the
grand, the (now) immaculate Cetchwayo.

To have combined the charity of a bishop with
the military science of "one who knows war well,"
would have been so delightful as to be cheaply
purchased at the price of a few hundred lives.

We should not indeed have been the "laughing-stock of Europe," at least not until a month after we had become an object of contempt to Africa, while the Swazis and Sekukuni would have been in a broad guffaw for several weeks ere "the foreign critics" had learnt by telegraph how great a jest had been prepared for them by "one who knows that what he may write, etc."

To speak seriously, was there ever advanced a more feeble, foolish, dangerous proposal than this, to push forward into an almost unknown country detachments tied down to the protection of convoys, and unprovided with any means for exploration or reconnaissance? Their fate must have been the same as that of the unlucky company which was destroyed near Luneburg.

If the detachment were strong enough to protect the convoy, it would also be so numerous as to eat it up; if it were small enough to leave a remnant of stores for a depôt, then both convoy and escort would have been eaten up by the Zulus.

The plan of "one who knows war well" is inadmissible, and we cannot but feel that the time which Lord Chelmsford spent in preparing everything for his advance (long as it may have seemed to some*) was well employed, while his determina-

* It was about six weeks; namely, from the 20th April (when he returned from Etshowe) to the 30th of June.

tion not to move till all was ready was wise and
prudent, and reaped its due reward at last in the
rapidity with which success crowned his efforts,
when in the fulness of time he marched on Ulundi.

(iv.) The tactics at Ulundi.

Of these Mr. Forbes, since they were successful,
has little to say, though he cannot restrain himself
from the sneer of "great good fortune."

The reason why Colonel Wood was not sent
"across the river . . . to occupy the Kopje"
was that a reconnaissance having been made of the
ground by that officer and Colonel Buller, they reported that it was unfit for fighting purposes.

Another sneer—" It was a soldier's, and not a
general's fight;" so, in the sense that there was but
little tactical manœuvring, were Waterloo, Talavera,
Busaco, and Albuera; so was the Alma; so, above
all, was Inkermann; so, indeed, have been most of
the victories obtained by British troops, who have
usually won by sheer fighting power and not by
tactical skill, for which, indeed, there was no scope
at Ulundi.

"While it lasted, Lord Chelmsford was every
inch a soldier," smacks of the war correspondent,
and we are glad to meet him again without dis-
guise.

Mr. Forbes, omitting Colonel Buller's distin-

guished corps, says that only three squadrons of
cavalry were present out of the two regiments,
which he styles a brigade, and that the remainder
was "frittered away" along the frontier, the
defence of which Lord Chelmsford had previously
"shunned almost entirely." Which course would
Mr. Forbes have preferred—that the frontier
should have been denuded of cavalry at the time
of the commencement of the advance, or that Lord
Chelmsford should have waited before fighting
until the cavalry was ready to join him? The
former would have been impossible, as, even on
half rations, only the three squadrons could be
foraged, while the latter would have troubled the
"unofficial person" as grievously as the general's
supposed intention to wait for Crealock.

4th Period. From the combat of Ulundi until
Lord Chelmsford's resignation of the command.

Mr. Forbes's charge is as follows :—That, after
the victory of Ulundi, Lord Chelmsford, by withdrawing his force from its forward position, "threw
to the wind" the results of the battle.

Let us first dismiss in a few words the statement
that "Lord Chelmsford, on the afternoon of the
battle, retired his force into the laager on the
Umvaloosi." This merely means that the men
returned to their dinners, in place of waiting on

4

the battle-field until the camp was brought to
them.

"Ulundi was but a means to an end ; that end
. . . was a satisfactory peace and the capture of
Cetchwayo."

The latter Mr. Forbes insists on, and perhaps with reason, though the fact that King
Coffee was never even seen, far less captured, did
not diminish the honours gained in the Ashantee
war.   But, granting that Cetchwayo's capture was
a necessity, did it not directly result from the battle
of Ulundi, which dispersed his army beyond recall,
and forced him as a fugitive into pathless forests ?

On the other hand, let us consider how the case
would have stood if Lord Chelmsford had remained
at Ulundi.   His infantry would have been useless,
his cavalry were too few for the purpose of catch-
ing Cetchwayo, who was far away from the field
before the battle was over, and this useless force
must have been fed from the frontier.

The facts stand thus : after the battle of Ulundi,
Lord Chelmsford withdrew his victorious force to
a position where they could be more easily supplied, and Sir Garnet Wolseley pushed on a force
of cavalry, which, after about six weeks, captured
the king.

Mr. Forbes says : " If 20,000 Zulus attacked
Lord Chelmsford at Ulundi, and if 2,000 of them
were put *hors de combat*, manifestly 18,000 re-

mained available for further mischief at the bidding of the monarch." This is nonsense, and Mr. Forbes knows that it is so ; for the 18,000 were scattered, weary of fighting, and could never have been united into an army. Hear Cetchwayo on the subject :* " If to-morrow there should be another battle, you will all run away ; and the whites will follow, and capture me only."

Nothing remained of the Zulu army after Ulundi, and Lord Chelmsford retired knowing that he *had* " fully accomplished the object for which he advanced," and that the hunting of the king required, not an army, but a number of detachments under subordinate officers.

The capture of Cetchwayo was a necessary consequence of Ulundi, but a satisfactory peace depended, and depends, on other factors. Peace was made possible by Ulundi, but not even Mr. Forbes can tell us what may make it satisfactory.

Lord Chelmsford had, let us say, provisions for a fortnight ; but would a fortnight have sufficed for the capture of Cetchwayo, and what supplies were on the way to the army ? What was to happen at the end of that fortnight ? The choice lay between a leisurely retirement on the 5th of July, and a precipitate retreat a fortnight later under pressure of hunger : 500 cavalry worked during six weeks to catch Cetchwayo, and the pre-

* " Cetchwayo's Dutchman," page 55.

4—2

sence of 10,000 infantry at Ulundi would not have shortened that term by one hour.

The results of Ulundi were, the utter destruction of the Zulu army as a body, the consequent opening up of Zululand to small detachments of troops, and the ultimate capture of Cetchwayo ; and, far from involving the country in needless expenditure, Lord Chelmsford probably saved money as well as lives by withdrawing his now unnecessarily large force from Ulundi, $87\frac{1}{2}$ miles from Port Durnford (a very long distance for "*six* marches"), and by placing it where it could be more easily supplied, while, at the same time, his retirement, since no Zulu resistance was then possible, did not in any way prevent the incursions and searchings of small bodies of troops.

What is Mr. Forbes's idea of Lord Chelmsford's duty under the circumstances ? Ought he to have plunged with 3,000 infantry into an unknown forest, lengthening and subdividing his communications day by day ? or should he have remained encamped at Ulundi, while his stores daily diminished, merely for the purpose of affording moral support (for physical support was impossible) to small bodies of cavalry, several miles in advance, in pursuit of a broken and dispersed enemy ? Nothing but the blindness born of an injured vanity could make any man believe such a course to be wise or right.

Mr. Forbes does not state that he has *seen* " the correspondence which at this time passed between Lord Chelmsford and his superior officer," and it is preferable to assume that he is speaking on hearsay rather than to suppose that any officer has so slight a conception of military honour that he would permit the perusal of such communica-cations.

Be this as it may, the notion that Lord Chelmsford could be put upon his trial before a court-martial is so ludicrous, that we can believe it to be the opinion of Mr. Forbes that such a thing is possible, only on the supposition that his know-ledge of law is as vague as his knowledgeof war.

Accusation the last. That Colonel Wood's column was not allowed to " cut Zululand in two " by marching on Utrecht. What possible object could such a march have had ? It would have been a triumphal progress among women and children, for the Zulus were now scattered, their king a fugitive, their army a rabble, and their military kraals deserted or burnt, while by this procession the amount of ground which had to be covered by Colonel Wood's force before embarkation would have been trebled.

If there had been the smallest attempt at re-sistance to the capture of the king, this part of Mr. Forbes's article might be intelligible, but there was not even a protest against it, and of the

18,000 who escaped from Ulundi, a poor twenty were with Cetchwayo when he was captured. Mr. Forbes at the last propounds a species of riddle; and as we are not " called upon to guess at the solution of a conundrum," we are entitled to ask him what that is which, " save in actual fighting, is, to all intents and purposes, a campaign " ?   Such a marvel, if described with Mr. Forbes's usual spirit, should form a valuable contribution to the proceedings of the Peace Society, and the author might look forward with security to the ultimate possession of the sinecure appointment of War Correspondent during the Millennium.

In conclusion, I wish to state that, in the preceding pages, I have been careful to assert nothing as a fact for which I cannot produce convincing proof, either by the evidence of officers, or from official documents.

I may perhaps be permitted to mention that I have no personal acquaintance with Lord Chelmsford, nor was I present in Africa during the Zulu war, and that I have no interest in writing this paper, except such as all must feel who have regretted to see a gallant officer and an honourable gentleman placed in a false position by the snarls of a self-styled Military Critic.

THE END.

9 781845 748951